LET YOUR WORD BE YOUR WORD

JEFFREY T TIERNEY

Jeffrey T. Tierney

Let Your Word Be Your Word

Sound Mind Books

www.jeffreytierney.org

Requests for information should be sent to:

soundmindjt@gmail.com

ISBN: 979-8-9912153-0-5

❀ Created with Vellum

CONTENTS

INTRODUCTION

We have entered a critical time in our world where the enemy, the principalities, powers, and rulers of this world keep us locked in a constant state of fear. Individuals, parents, families, and children are exhausted from the pressures of life.

In my work as a social service employee for over 20 years, and in getting my life and heart together in Jesus, I have learned that most of us do not have our priorities established. We lack critical skills such as focus and discipline.

Satan will use worldly things to distract us from our Book of Life purpose that God has designed for each of us to pursue.

~

Psalm 139:16 - "Your eyes saw my substance, being yet unformed. In Your book they all were written, the days fashioned for me, when as yet there were none of them."

Often, we get lost in doing things that will not matter in the end because we are tired, stressed, and not putting God first. We have to become obedient and comfortable turning every area of our lives over to God so He can help us transform those areas. The more I walk with Jesus, the more I learn He is interested in helping us with our relationships, finances, life purpose, health, exercising, kids, spouse, emotional, spiritual life, and mental well-being, or forgiveness. No area is off limits to Him. He is interested. We only have to commit to Him and turn ourselves into Him daily.

However, whenever we are numb or refuse to take accountability or see that there is even an issue within ourselves or our relationships, we are unable to be effective individuals for our Book of Life Purpose, Christ, our loved ones, others, as a church. We are ineffective for standing up against the anti-life agendas that are displayed in every institution. Our spiritual vision is clouded, and we become lost in the chaos and darkness, whether we are aware of this or not.

This is where people need to start asking for discernment in these areas. As *John 10:10* states," **The thief does not come except to steal, and to kill, and to destroy."** Over the past several years, it has been interesting for me to watch individuals inside and outside of the church get caught up in the Spirit of deception.

In the book *Mesmerize* by David Edwards, the following quote sums up where individuals and the church need overall discernment for everything happening right now on this earth. **"Heaven on earth is always redemptive. Hell on earth is always destructive. Each will be known by the fruit it bears. If it brings life abundantly, its origin is Jesus—the**

Restorer of the Plan, Repairer of the Breach. If it steals, kills, and destroys, then it's a perversion from the fallen one—the accuser and slanderer. If you're unsure of the origin, follow the fruit: did it create or pervert?"

When believers begin to do this, *Matthew 16:18-20* will become effective - *"And I also say to you that you are Peter, and on this rock, I will build My church, and the gates of Hades shall not prevail against it. And I will give you the keys of the Kingdom of Heaven, and whatever you bind on earth will be bound in Heaven, and whatever you loose on earth will be loosed in Heaven."*

When I wrote *The Love Well Letters*, I was close to death. I wanted to share my experience and what I learned. The reason for this short book is to, once again, share with you my realization that we need more people in the church to follow through on the guidance of the Holy Spirit so that we create a ripple effect for the Kingdom of God to counteract the darkness of this world. Making empty promises can have massive implications for the Kingdom of God, other people's ministries, and how the Holy Spirit wants to work through others to help people on this earth. The goal is not to shame, guilt, condemn, or make one do things out of compulsion. It is about shining a light on the enemy's agenda to keep us stuck in activities that will mean nothing. The goal is to inspire us to our deepest calling to love others well and to bring others hope, not to glorify ourselves but our Heavenly Father, and to show why we are to be the salt of the earth and to carry out Christ's greatest command-ment. As *John 13:34-35 states, "A new commandment I give to you, that you love one another; as I have loved you, that you also love one another. By this all will know that you are My disciples, if you have love for one another.* When we do this, you will be surprised how much love flows in your life and how the Kingdom of God moves in your own life as well as the lives of others. May the Trinity guide you throughout this process, to heal what needs to be healed, to have you operating in alignment with the perfect will of God to complete your Book of Life Purpose, to serve those who God deems appropriate, and for you to act with boldness and courage, when Jesus commands you to do so, in Jesus' Name.

"If any of you lacks wisdom, let him ask of God, who gives to all liberally and without reproach, and it will be given to him. But let him ask in faith, with no doubting, for he who doubts is like a wave of the sea driven and tossed by the wind. For let not that man suppose that he will receive anything from the Lord; he is a double-minded man, unstable in all his ways." – James 1:5-8

~

I want to dedicate this book to my father. My relationship was often difficult with you, but in a sense, I see the goodness and things that God equipped you to do on this earth that were never fully realized. I see your attention to detail, precision, not cutting corners, accountability, and serving others as gifts you have given me as I have grown older. I have seen you do the best you could as a father to prepare for things that might happen. These are critical skills that we need in these times, and I appreciate you doing the best you could to pass these skills on to me. More than ever, I see your talents and gifts aiding me as the man I am to be on this earth.

I would also like to dedicate this book to the people who never followed through on the things I had asked and needed so I could learn the importance of being a man of my word, not breaking my promises, and bringing the gift of consistency. I am not perfect, and I still sin and miss the mark. However, I realize it is a pleasure to be obedient to the Lord and follow through on what He asks me to do for His glory.

Finally, thank you to all the individuals who helped me physically, mentally, emotionally, spiritually, financially, and relationally. You have taught me also how to love and give back. Cassandra Steele, thank you for teaching me of what it means to be the Salt of the Earth.

1

———

WHAT WOULD YOU DO IF YOU HAD ONE WEEK TO LIVE?

In the movie, *One Week*, Joshua Jackson is diagnosed with a terminal cancer. Instead of seeking cancer treatment, he decides to go on a motorcycle trip across Canada to find out the deeper meaning of life.

I know that when I was very sick, this movie had a very personal meaning to me. It started to get me to think about leaving a legacy, being a solid man, and living with purpose and accountability. While I was thinking of all these things that I could be, I was still living in the new and occult at the time and had not yet been born again to Jesus Christ, my Lord and Savior.

I realize that this movie was a steppingstone that would begin to prepare me on my journey to start really living from my Book of Life Purpose, stop making excuses, find ways to better my health, and start looking for ways out of financial turmoil. I felt hampered by medical negligence, but I didn't want to remain a victim. This movie began to ask me challenging questions. What would I do if I had one week left to live? How would I spend it? Whom would I spend my time with? How would I give to others, follow through consistently, and not make excuses? With being given a 70 percent chance of not surviving my heart surgery to remove an PFO Septal Occluder Device that was causing several heart and neurological issues due to metal allergies discussed in detail in the *The Love Well Letters*, I began to push myself on where I wanted to be as a man and as a person in 5 years. I didn't want to leave anything unsaid or undone when I left this earth. All of these events and trials would prepare me for coming back to Christ and preparing for biblical understanding several years later.

CHAPTER 1 QUESTIONS for Prayer and Deliverance with the Holy Spirt, Jesus, and the Heavenly Father:

1. If you only had one week left to live, what are the 3 areas you would want immediate correction to extend your life?
2. What areas do you feel that you have pride in that keep you from being obedient to follow what the Lord asks you to do for your life calling or do for others? Is it fear or the fear of being rejected? What are the factors stopping you? If you had one week to live, would this be easier for you to do for yourself and others?
3. If you only had one week left to live, how would you be obedient to God in communicating your love and doing things for yourself and others?

IN CLOSING, I ask all of you to work with the Holy Spirit on this for a week. So many of us get bogged down by the world's heaviness, and we don't live with intention and purpose. Again, I want to be clear that I do not want to speak death over, but how could this then benefit you from living this consistently for yourself, Christ, others, and those you love dearly?

2

———

THE DECISION TO COMMIT

W hat makes commitment to God, Christ, the Word of God, developing character, and loving others such a difficult task to complete in these times? Why is self-discipline so hard to come by? I have asked myself this question for over 20 years. The answer isn't as simple as we might always think. I have concluded that it is several areas.

First, we are fighting a spiritual battle in this realm more than most realize. If people understood what Satan and his minions (both human and non-human forms) were doing to us, they would revolt in a heartbeat because they would not put up with it. People have observed corruption at every level of most institutions during the last two years. What is stunning is that when real truth does emerge, those voices are silenced. Any person with any sense of rational intelligence and the spiritual gift of discernment should be able to see through the darkness behind these false narratives. Jesus was very specific in Matthew 16:18-20 when He said, ***"And I also say to you that you are Peter, and on this rock, I will build My church, and the gates of Hades shall not prevail*** *against it. And I will give you the keys of the Kingdom of Heaven, and whatever you bind on earth¹will be bound in Heaven, and whatever you lose on earth will be lost in Heaven."* We have been under tremendous pressure and have had fear thrown at us from all directions. That is why committing to God's Words and understanding how the Spirit of fear operates is crucial. Renewing your mind daily in the Word of God is the first step, quieting yourself in prayer with God is the second step, and getting clear on what matters is the third step. Asking for wisdom and discernment on the truth of what is happening in all circumstances is something that needs to happen all of the time.

One thing that stops people from committing to being obedient to God is their past wounds and traumas. We are made up of a born-again spirit, a soul (mind, will, and emotions), and a body. When we are hurt, the aftermath, or the trauma, sticks to us like black goo. Words, thoughts, or belief systems begin to shape us, and we react based on those falsehoods instead of what the Word of God says about us. Jesus Christ has delivered us through his death on the cross. He has restored us to victory. Romans 8:11 tells us, *"If the Spirit of Him who raised Jesus from the dead dwells in you, He who raised Christ from the dead will also give life to your mortal bodies¹through His Spirit who dwells in you."*

What does this mean? The same power that raised Jesus from the dead can heal our bodies and our minds. I believe it can heal anything within our broken selves. We need to be willing to turn ourselves into the Lord, as Dr. Kevin Zadai says, and be willing to be honest with the Lord. We need not be afraid of correction. The Lord and the Holy Spirit can speed up the healing process and offer an alternative so that we live in sync with the Lord's plan for our lives.

As I continue to grow and mature, I am learning that

these are all tests to see how willing I am to surrender myself to Christ. How willing am I to let go of pride and be the man God wants me to be (refer to Psalm 139:16). It's not always easy. Sometimes, there is pushback from fear or the Spirit of rejection. Often, the demons do not want us to be free. Again, discernment is key.

I never really understood how the Spirit of fear operated until I started to examine 1 Corinthians 10:13. *"No temptation has overtaken you except such as is common to man; but God is faithful, who will not allow you to be tempted beyond what you are able, but with the temptation will also make the way of escape, that you may be able to bear it."*

Jesus came to set us free. He does not want us to suffer. The church has failed to teach us to repent or realize that demonic oppression goes on more often than not. We have to take accountability in using the Word of God and taking authority in Jesus to cast Satan and his minions out of our lives. When we focus on the fact that we are a new creation in Christ, we can follow God's plan clearly and directly and be obedient to what He asks us to do for Him and His Kingdom.

The final thing I have noticed that can take a toll on a person is the overall health of one's body. Sometimes, certain foods need to be eliminated from a person's routine. Often, certain minerals, supplements, exercise or removing certain products can also be the answer. We are living in a world where we are bombarded by chemicals and poisons coming from several institutions. I encourage each person to do his or her research and ask the Holy Spirit what needs to be removed or added. Sometimes, we have generational curses or patterns that must be dealt with in our bloodline. Pray for discernment and correction from the Lord. He is our healing. Today, more than ever, there is a coordinated attack on our health from the most trusted institutions on the planet, and again, this is where discernment needs to be used.

Two scriptures come to me consistently in these end times. First, Matthew 24:24 states, *"False christs and false prophets will rise and show great signs and wonders to deceive, if possible, even the elect."* Ask yourself if every new great discovery aligns with scripture. If things have multiple side effects, do you think this comes from God or the enemy? Jesus went about doing His Father's business, healing, not harming. We need discernment in those things no matter what they promise to do. Nothing should ever alter our original DNA blueprint of how God created us.

The second scripture coming to me in these end-day times is 1 Corinthians 6:19: *"Or do you not know that your body is the temple of the Holy Spirit who is in you, whom you have from God, and you are not your own?"* Over the past year, I have learned to stop giving myself excuses for what I say to myself, what I put into my body, or how hard I push myself. If I do not take care of the body that God gave me, I will not be on this earth. That is why I must partner with the Holy Spirit on what I must do to care for my physical body properly.

CHAPTER 2 QUESTIONS for Prayer and Deliverance with the Holy Spirt, Jesus, and the Heavenly Father:

1. What areas of your life is the enemy tormenting you in? Are you willing to ask the Holy Spirit to reveal the enemies' battle plan against you so you

can start walking your Book of Life purpose out on this earth and be obedient to God's calling?

2. What areas of your life do you need to clean up in the areas of trauma or soul wounds that prevent you from walking in your Spirit? What stops you from doing this work? What keeps you numbed out? How would your life change if you committed to working on your heart with the Lord?

3. What areas of your life do you need to develop physically? What does your relationship with discernment look like?

3

CLOSING THE GAPS, DEFINING YOUR PRIORITIES!

As we walk through the end days, it becomes more evident that individuals and families are consistently in survival mode. It seems like it is harder to thrive due to concerns over income, wars, disease, and lack of mentality. Don't be fooled, as this is done on purpose by Satan in using people in positions of power to keep us stressed out and in the mindset of lack. I am not perfect in my understanding of relying on God. I still get into my will of trying to figure things out on my own. However, my goal is to be in the complete Will of God, to turn everything over to Him and to walk side by side with Him.

Until I get an answer to act on something, I will do as Proverbs 3:5-6 instructs, ***"Trust in the LORD with all your heart, and lean not on your own understanding. In all your ways acknowledge Him, and He shall direct your paths."*** Patience can often be difficult when we are stressed or burnt out from not pursuing our life purpose, health, trauma, relationship problems, or financial difficulties. Whatever the issue may be, we can often feel defeated, especially when the enemy consistently fires his darts toward us.

I found out recently that when I am not aligned with God's calling for my life, I feel resentment or bitterness, which is not what God is calling me to do. I do my best to obey what Jesus asks me to do for myself and others. I would ask the Holy Spirit for correction on what needed to change in me or what correction I needed to align with God's will. Sometimes, deliverance from the enemy was required. Other times, belief systems were getting in the way. Often, I needed quiet to check in and see if it was the correct timing to move forward with things.

Patience also becomes difficult when you feel that you or others might be suffering. That is when we need to stand tall in the Word of God and declare His promises just as Jesus did to Satan in the desert. Luke 4:4 states, *"But Jesus answered him, saying it is written, that man shall not live by bread only, but by every word of God."* Thus, it is crucial that when we feel weary and defeated, we go to the Word of God to renew our minds. We do as Joshua 1:8 instructs: *"This Book of the Law shall not depart from your mouth, but you shall meditate in it day and night, that you may observe to do according to all that is written in it. For then you will make your way prosperous, and then you will have good success."* I have learned that I must devote my time to God first thing in the morning. I will admit, sometimes, due to fatigue or long work days, I can get thrown off my routine for 1 to 3 days a week every so often, but if I do not get myself in line with the Lord, I start to see other areas of my life unravel quickly. To me, this is a non-negotiable area. I must begin and end my days with quiet, scripture, and prayer with God.

How do we begin then to define our priorities and close the gaps to walking in our Book of Life purpose with the Heavenly Father? I often ask myself and others, "Do you ever find yourself in quiet or busy moments where you feel the Holy Spirit, Jesus, or your Heavenly Father asking you to do something, and you don't follow through? Perhaps it is learning a new skill, getting a new job, or starting to exercise. A great place to begin understanding what needs to be prioritized in your life is to start listening to a voice we frequently ignore.

I always like to break things down in terms of physical, mental, emotional, spiritual, financial, life purpose, and relationship levels. However, I go to the Trinity with these concerns. I know I am meant to succeed and prosper in these areas. If I am not aligned in all these areas, how can I be an effective weapon for the Kingdom of God? I cannot. I ask for refinement daily and keep working on my heart and correction with the Lord. We all need to get to a place where we can become non-defensive and thrive instead of survive.

Practice and repetition are essential. It takes learning your authority in Jesus. It takes facing your fears, leaving your past behind, doing new things that might scare you, and knowing you can do new things. It may require acquiring new skills or getting help and being delivered from demonic oppression. 1 John 4:18 states, "***There is no fear in love, but perfect love casts out fear because fear involves torment. But he who fears has not been made perfect in love.***" We all have been in places where we feel that Spirit of fear, demonic torment, and oppression. I experience days filled with fear, but that is where I have had to learn authority in Jesus and know the power of His redemptive Blood. We must get our priorities straight and be disciplined to withstand the enemy.

CHAPTER 3 QUESTIONS for Prayer and Deliverance with the Holy Spirt, Jesus, and the Heavenly Father:

1. What are the things you continue to put off that you know you need to complete to align your life with God on physical, mental, emotional, spiritual, financial, life purpose, and relationship levels? What makes you resist following through on what God calls you to do on these levels? Is it fear? Is it simple health or dietary things that need to be changed? Is it demonic oppression? Are they strongholds? Go to the Holy Spirit in prayer and ask what is holding you back from achieving God's Book of Life purpose for you in each of these areas and what God's battle plan for your deliverance.

2. What are the areas of life that you are passionate about? Do you have a disciplined schedule that you stick to daily and weekly? I have learned that there are seasons where we will do more or less. The key is to build up small wins and to be consistent.

3. Finally, ask the Holy Spirit about the first areas you can begin to work on to align with God's plan for your life. What small steps can you take so you don't get overwhelmed, quit and give up? When I first started writing and exercising, I set tiny goals. Mondays were set aside for a 30-minute writing session. Nothing interrupted that time, and I set boundaries with people. As I mastered that, I eventually added another day in the week for the same amount of time. As I learned that, I began feeling peace and aligned

with God's purpose for my life. They were small wins that gave me the confidence that I could win and that the Holy Spirit was directing me. I also picked two days a week to exercise, with only a 20-minute target, so I would not give up. As I mastered this for a month, I increased my mileage and time to stay consistent. Small goals build consistency and give you the confidence in the Lord. Jesus has the best plans to help us if we only go to Him and submit.

4

RECEIVING OUR DAILY BREAD
FROM OUR FATHER ABBA

When I reflect on some of my brushes with death and being involved in the new age and occult, I often think of the lines from U2's song, "Lights of Home." The lyrics say, "Shouldn't be here cause I should be dead. I can see the lights in front of me. I believe my best days are ahead. I can see the lights in front of me. Oh, Jesus, if I'm still your friend, what the heck you got for me? I gotta get out from under my bed to see again the lights in front of me. I've been waiting a long time to get home." I am reminded of when Jesus visits and heals the man who had been waiting at Sheep's Gate, at the pool of Bethesda. He asks him in John 5, *"Do you want to be made well?' Jesus said to him, 'Rise, take up your bed and walk.' And immediately, the man was made well, took up his bed, and walked. Afterward, Jesus found him in the temple and said to him, 'See, you have been made well. Sin no more, lest a worse thing come upon you.'"*

Sometimes, we forget how simple Jesus's instructions are regarding healing. We must shift our mindsets or belief systems as followers and believers. Sin has played a role in my illness or circumstances, and I have had to repent, something that Satan has lured the church away from teaching in these current times. We do have to repent and humble ourselves for correction out of Fear of the Lord, and to become closer, and to do as Peter 1:15-16 instructs us, *"but as He who called you is holy, you also be holy in all your conduct, because it is written, 'Be holy, for I am holy.'"* 2 Peter 1:4 also encourages us to practice the following, *"By which have been given to us exceedingly great and precious promises, that through these you may be partakers of the divine nature, having escaped the corruption that is in the world through lust."*

Jesus encourages us to reach out to our Father to receive our daily blessings. Part of what I am asking my readers to realize is that when we become lukewarm or inconsistent, there are patterns that we need to become aware of in this earthly realm. Is it a physical issue that exercise, minerals, vitamins, or nutrition can correct? Is it a soul wound, a trauma that has been caused to the mind, will, emotions, or belief systems, that needs to be dealt with? Is this a spiritual or demonic oppression issue where we need some deliverance or to use our authority in Jesus's name? The only way we can begin to sift through the complexities of these questions is by reading the Word of God, praying in the Spirit, and in silence with God.

We have to escape the noise as Jesus did in the Gospels. He would leave to spend time and connect with His heavenly Father. We need to be intentional about investing in the Trinity. When we find that areas of our lives are in chaos, we discipline ourselves and become almost militant to turn everything over to God for immediate correction. We must choose to get out of victim mode, take accountability, and face truths about ourselves that may be unpleasant. Satan and his minions want us to stay stuck in whatever is keeping us sick, tired, numbed out, addicted, or unhealthy. However, when we take that quiet time and plug into the truth of what scripture declares us to be under God's creation and as His Kids, there is nothing He cannot free us from. It has already been done for us on the cross, and we can receive that freedom and healing. We have to be willing to go to the Lord without a sense of pride or arrogance. Sometimes, healing can happen instantly. I have seen that in my own life. However, it is often a process as the power of the Holy Spirit reveals more. When our ship goes off course, we must take the time to quiet ourselves to get the battle plan from our Commander in Chief [Jesus] and execute it for ourselves and those we love. We, in turn, create action rather than wallow in passivity. We learn accountability, which helps us hear God's voice on when and when not to act. If we refine this skill, wait patiently on the Lord, and not lean on our understanding, things will shift, and we will see movement. As Proverbs 16:9 states, ***"A man's heart plans his way, but the Lord directs his steps."*** I love Abbie Gamboa, a singer from the Upperroom. She sings the

song "Praise," and in the song's lyrics, she shouts, "Whatever you came in with tonight, just let it go."

As I close this section, I ask you to go to your prayer closet and become diligent when you feel stuck or off-course in essential areas of your life. Seek the Lord and stay consistent with your obedience practice to love others and be the best you can be for the Lord while serving His Kingdom. ~~~~~

Chapter 4 Questions for Prayer and Deliverance with the Holy Spirt, Jesus, and the Heavenly Father:

1. What makes it hard to have consistent quiet time with the Trinity? What is one step you would be willing to take immediately to put this into practice, even if it is just starting with 10 minutes, one day a week?

2. What areas do you find yourself consistently stumbling in that are holding you back from being obedient to the Lord and not seeing the fruits you know you are meant to produce for the Kingdom of Heaven on Earth? What is one small step you could take to start to address this? I would suggest learning about what an emotionally safe and unsafe person. Refer to Dr. Henry Cloud's *Safe People: How to Find Relationships that are Good for You and Avoid Those That Aren't.*

3. Ask the Holy Spirit to reveal the areas holding you back on physical, mental, emotional, spiritual, life purpose, financial, and relationship levels.

5

LEAVING THE VICTIM CARD BEHIND

One of the main things that keeps individuals side-lined to being obedient to God, following through on His Word, and carrying out what He wants us to do is being stuck in the evil and trauma that has been carried out against us. We cannot operate in sync with Heaven if we have pain in our souls. It prevents us from moving forward in our lives and moving forward in the direction that Christ planned for us in our Book of Life (Refer to Psalm 139:16).

God is still pruning the vines within me to make me a complete Kingdom Man. 3 John 1:2-14 states, *"Beloved, I pray that you may prosper in all things and be in health, just as your soul prospers. For I rejoiced greatly when brethren came and testified of the truth that is in you, just as you walk in the truth. I have no greater joy than to hear that my children walk in truth."* We are to prosper in all areas of life with Jesus, and He is our ultimate healer. Isaiah 61:3 has always been a calming scripture for me when I have felt troubled, *"He wants me to help those in Zion who are filled with sorrow. I will put beautiful crowns on their heads in place of ashes. I will anoint them with olive oil to give them joy instead of sorrow. I will give them a spirit of praise in place of a spirit of sadness. They will be like oak trees that are strong and straight. The LORD himself will plant them in the land. That will show how glorious he is."*

To me, Jesus truly knows and understands what trauma is. He was beaten, bruised, whipped, killed, and took on all of our sins for us. He purchased and redeemed us because He loved us. He knew what it was like to be betrayed and to feel that sense of abandonment at the very last moments of His life on the cross. He cried, "Abba, why have you forsaken me." He knew what it was like when he asked his disciples to pray with Him in the garden as he was about to be arrested, and they could not stay awake. He knew that Peter would deny Him, and Judas would betray him. He knew the ultimate pain of betrayal, yet He kept calm amid the storm.

Jesus knows better than any human how to calm our pain and fears and wipe away our deepest pain and sorrows. As I have dealt with some of my past, I have asked Jesus how to be more like Him. It is crucial to go to in humility, not shame, and ask for help. Some scholars believe the Bible refers to pride anywhere from 46 to 58 times. If we stay in pride, we cannot admit we have a problem or work toward resolving our inner conflicts or with others. We will continue to hurt others and our relationships if we remain in pride. We will grieve the Holy Spirit and the Lord; it does not need to be this way.

In ministry school, Dr. Kevin Zadai taught us to turn our hurt and sorrow over to Jesus in order to be free. The first step in being victim-free is learning how to forgive. When we can forgive others, we begin to get clarity from the Holy Spirit about mending the relationship. Perhaps we are the ones who need to change. Sometimes, we are called to put boundaries down for ourselves or asked to walk away because the relationship does not honor ourselves or God. Both individuals must be committed to walking toward God and showing love to one another daily. As Matthew 6:14-15 points out, *"For if you forgive men their trespasses, your heavenly Father will also forgive you. But if you do not forgive men their trespasses, neither will your Father forgive your trespasses."* Forgiveness is the first key to stepping out of victimhood.

The second step to walking out of victimhood is accepting accountability for everything in your life. In prayer, God has given me personal insight that He has never wanted me to fail. He has always been with me and wanted me to succeed. Some of me going erratic and not listening to Him have resulted in the choices and places I am in. That is why repenting and becoming obedient have become critical in my walk over the past two years. When I try to take control, disaster usually happens shortly after. As I have learned to walk side by side with Jesus and have developed more patience, things tend to work out more favorably for me and others.

Taking accountability for my belief systems, thoughts, and actions has changed everything in my life. I cannot force others to operate in that same manner, but if I can walk with the Lord and do as Proverbs 3:5-6 instructs, I will see better success in my life. *"Trust in the Lord with all your heart, and lean not on your own understanding. In all your ways acknowledge Him, and He shall direct your paths."*

The last thing I have learned is learning my identity in Christ and that we are to walk under the authority of Jesus. The enemy does not want many Christians to know this. I recommend Dr. Kevin Zadai's book, *The Mystery of Power Words*, as it will help you dig deeper into that authority.

CHAPTER 5 QUESTIONS for Prayer and Deliverance with the Holy Spirt, Jesus, and the Heavenly Father:

1. What benefits do you get from staying stuck in the victim mentality or playing the victim card?
2. Define your identity in Christ. We all have different roles to play in this life. For example, you may be a teacher, a husband, or a wife. You may be a student. If those were taken away, what would be left?
3. Get quiet and go to the Lord in prayer. Ask Him to reveal the areas of your life where you are stuck as a victim. How is it impacting your life? Ask for the steps to begin to heal these wounds so you can move forward.

6

COMING INTO AGREEMENT WITH GOD

We obey God's will when we apply John 5:19 into action. ***"Then Jesus answered and said to them, "Most assuredly, I say to you, the Son can do nothing of Himself, but what He sees the Father do; for whatever He does, the Son also does in like manner."*** When we meditate on this scripture, each of us, as Sons and Daughters of the King, can begin to align with what God asks us to do for His kingdom on earth. We stop making excuses and begin each day in His Word, asking Him how we can carry out His will throughout the day. If the Lord asks us to complete a task for the day, we follow through on those orders. We agree with Him by following His plan for our lives and serving others for His Kingdom. We are His children and ambassadors on this earth. We are on "display" as Dr. Kevin Zadai states, for His glory; serving and completing His will daily is a pleasure.

When we obey, He will shower us with peace, completion, and alignment. We can rest knowing that we were obedient, and others may carry out His will by executing the Father's will. They may be one step closer to healing, learning a new skill, starting a business, turning away from sin, or feeling value. The possibilities are endless in the kingdom of God. Matthew 19:26 states, **"But Jesus looked at them and said to them, "With men this is impossible, but with God all things are possible."**

As I have grown closer in my walk with God, I know that the Spirit of fear and rejection kept me from taking small steps at the beginning of my journey. When I dug deeper into the Word, worked with my pastor, and entered ministry school, I realized that no matter how small of steps I was taking, at least it was something for God. The Spirit of fear had me trapped because of the medical bankruptcies I had to endure. I felt I could not do things on the level my heart envisioned, so I let myself stay stuck in the ditch of wanting to help others financially. One night, while praying, I talked with Jesus. I told him that I knew what it felt like not to have simple things, that I was learning how to be a good steward with my money, and that I did not want to let medical incompetency and negligence ruin my life and the joy of giving to others. Luke 7:36-50 helped me deal with the shame and guilt of my past, take small steps to follow my Book of Life Purpose and be obedient to God as much as I could on a physical, mental, emotional, spiritual, relationship, and financial level. I was able to turn over everything to God. I thought that if I could take one small step and have one small victory, those tiny wins could build on one another. **"Then one of the Pharisees asked Him to eat with him. And He went to the Pharisee's house and sat down to eat. And behold, a woman in the city who was a sinner, when she knew that Jesus sat at the table in the Pharisee's house, brought an alabaster flask of fragrant oil, and stood at His feet behind Him weeping; and she began to wash His feet with her tears, and wiped them with the hair of her head, and she kissed**

His feet and anointed them with the fragrant oil. Now, when the Pharisee who had invited Him saw this, he spoke to himself, saying, 'This Man, if He were a prophet, would know who and what manner of woman this is who is touching Him, for she is a sinner.' And Jesus answered and said to him, 'Simon, I have something to say to you.' So, he said, 'Teacher, say it.' 'There was a certain creditor who had two debtors. One owed five hundred denarii and the other fifty. And when they had nothing with which to repay, he freely forgave them both. Tell Me, therefore, which of them will love him more?' Simon answered and said, 'I suppose the one whom he forgave more.' And He said to him, 'You have rightly judged.' Then He turned to the woman and said to Simon, 'Do you see this woman? I entered your house; you gave Me no water for My feet, but she has washed My feet with her tears and wiped them with the hair of her head. You gave Me no kiss, but this woman has not ceased to kiss My feet since the time I came in. You did not anoint My head with oil, but this woman has anointed My feet with fragrant oil. Therefore, I say to you, her sins, which are many, are forgiven, for she loved much. But to whom little is forgiven, the same loves little.' Then He said to her, 'Your sins are forgiven.' And those who sat at the table with Him began to say to themselves, 'Who is this who even forgives sins?' Then He said to the woman, 'Your faith has saved you. Go in peace.'"

Again, at this moment, I realized that doing something small for Jesus and being obedient was better than taking no action. Satan was using the guilt and shame of my past to keep me stuck in fear and to stop me from using the gift that God gave me for His glory. When I would pray and ask who needed help, names were provided, and I would start to sew into those individuals' lives. My tithes or offerings would go toward those individuals, and it was always on target and needed. I understood those things at a very, very deep level from going without. It was my way to honor God and others. I told Jesus that if I could be used to help others stop their suffering, I was all in and that now was the time to act and not back down, a necessary step in my growth and healing.

When you obey God and walk in the Spirit, you will experience peace. I know there is a fear of going alone or people not understanding you. I have been there and felt this many times. However, in these last days and as I continue to work on things, the passage keeps coming to me daily when I may struggle with sin or want to turn to things because of stressors, which quickly pulls me out of my sin, ego, and pride. Matthew 7:21-23 keeps me in a constant state of the Fear of the Lord and wanting to refine my heart and character with Jesus: *"Not everyone who says to Me, 'Lord, Lord,' shall enter the kingdom of Heaven, but he who does the will of My Father in Heaven. Many will say to Me in that day, 'Lord, Lord, have we not prophesied in Your name, cast out demons in Your name, and done many wonders in Your name?' And then I will declare to them, 'I never knew you; depart from Me, you who practice lawlessness!'"*

Don't be afraid to turn your eyes to Jesus for help. Things will improve and get better. The church is lukewarm at this point, and we need to be true ambassadors of God and His Kingdom. Things will begin to escalate soon on this earth. Do everything you can to heal with the Lord, become accountable, and put on the armor of God.

CHAPTER 6: Questions for Prayer and Deliverance with the Holy Spirit, Jesus, and the Heavenly Father:

1. Meditate of the scripture of Matthew 25;14-30, on your gifts and talents. How are you squandering or not seeing your gifts and talents come to fruition for the Kingdom of

Heaven on Earth? Ask the Holy Spirit to have your talents bear fruit so you can produce for those you love and help others prosper in these times.

2. Mediate on the scripture of the prodigal son, Luke 15-32. In what ways have you felt lost or disconnected from God? What ways is God calling you back home to serve his kingdom? What ways do you feel like an orphan Spirit? Ask the Holy Spirit to show you how to heal your wounds that are keeping you from being welcomed back into the kingdom as a son or daughter of the Most-High.

3. Ask the Holy Spirit for areas of forgiveness that need to be dealt with that are keeping you in the state of Rebellion and from being obedient to God and His Life Plan for you.

7

———

THE HOLY COVENANT WITH GOD

We no longer have to debate that when Jesus gave His life for us on the cross, He purchased our lives back, and we now enjoy all of the benefits of God and His Kingdom. God's Word will always remain true, no matter what man attempts to do to twist or manipulate it. The enemy always wants to make us believe that what God promises us is false.

As I am going through challenging times, being without a car and being stuck and continuing to work my way out of medical debt, I believe, at times, that God will not take care of me. This is a lie, none other than from Satan himself. In order to get my heart and mind aligned with the truth of God's Word, I must first know that my belief system is wrong. God is good. He loves me. He is here for me.

I was led to the passage in Luke 11:11 in the middle of the night to start dealing with the voice of doubt about my current situation, *"So I say to you, ask, and it will be given to you; seek, and you will find; knock, and it will be opened to you. For everyone who asks receives, and he who seeks finds, and to him who knocks, it will be opened. If a son asks for bread from any father among you, will he give him a stone? Or if he asks for a fish, will he give him a serpent instead of a fish? Or if he asks for an egg, will he offer him a scorpion? If you then, being evil, know how to give good gifts to your children, how much more will your heavenly Father give the Holy Spirit to those who ask Him!"*

As I walk through this lesson, I must keep telling myself that God is for and with me. He wants me to continue to work. I need a car to drive. I have learned new financial skills. It was not my fault that a device placed inside my heart caused a reaction inside my body that led to financial ruin. I have done everything I can to learn new habits. I have learned, most importantly, that most things on this earth are only distractions and that each purchase I make should only help me to benefit Christ and his Kingdom, as well as others that I am to serve.

We are God's children and must rely on our Father for provision. At times, that means we take accountability for the mistakes we have made in the past. We become obedient for the Lord to lead us out of the desert and into the promised land in our lives so we can prosper and be true ambassadors for God and His Kingdom. This is not about glorifying ourselves; we are to represent Christ on Earth.

I must wait patiently, lean not on my understanding, and let others in the Kingdom of God help me. Trusting others is difficult for me as people have not followed through for me in the past. I am committed to be accountable and do my part, yet I must "Be still and know God, and let others help without rocking the boat, and depend completely on God in this situation."

My best weapon is to do as Ephesians 6:11 instructs: "Put on the full armor of God, so that I may be able to stand firm against the schemes of the devil." My job or lesson in this is to stand firm with the promises that the Word of God declares as truth and continue to declare those scriptures as I walk through a very tough lesson in my life.

As we walk through being obedient to God, I think of Psalms 91, standing on that sacred ground that Moses did with the Lord. We are to enter into a very sacred covenant with God. Obedience to Him and His ways does not mean losing out. We have everything to gain by walking with God and Jesus. There is nothing to fear and nothing to be ashamed of. When you have lost everything, it starts to toughen you up. You begin to learn the true character of God and mimic that character so you can "be the salt of the earth" to others. Entering into the stillness, where you feel the love of God, you are held in preciousness in the arms of Jesus.

We sometimes feel alone on our journey as people do not understand us. We are in a sacred covenant with Jesus and His Father. Jesus shed his blood and purchased us back at a price. I want to do everything I can to be obedient, not out of shame or performance. I see all the things that Christ has walked me through. I see the choices and mistakes that I have made, but I am focused. As Paul states in 2 Timothy 4:7-8, " *I have fought the good fight, I have finished the race, I have kept the faith. Finally, there is laid up for me the crown of righteousness, which the Lord, the righteous Judge, will give to me on that day, and not to me only but also to all who have loved His appearing.*" All we can do is to do our best and walk deeply in our covenant with the Lord daily.

CHAPTER 7: Questions for Prayer and Deliverance with the Holy Spirt, Jesus, and the Heavenly Father:

1. What is blocking you from having a deeper intimacy with the Father, Son, and Holy Spirit?

2. What areas of your life do you still need deliverance from that would block your covenant with the Father, Son, and Holy Spirit?

3. What areas need forgiveness, both with yourself and others?

8

BEING AN OBEDIENT AND CONSISTENT AMBASSADOR FOR GOD AND HIS KINGDOM!

We have arrived in the end days as 2 Timothy 3 predicted, *"But know this, that in the last days perilous times will come: For men will be lovers of themselves, lovers of money, boasters, proud, blasphemers, disobedient to parents, unthankful, unholy, unloving, unforgiving, slanderers, without self-control, brutal, despisers of good, traitors, headstrong, haughty, lovers of pleasure rather than lovers of God, having a form of godliness but denying its power. And from such people turn away! For of this sort are those who creep into households and make captives of gullible women loaded down with sins, led away by various lusts, always learning and never able to come to the knowledge of the truth."*

When we begin to get our priorities straight and become obedient to God and His Kingdom, doing what we are told for our own Book of Life Purpose and helping others become the only things that matter. We get out of displaying these belief systems and behaviors mentioned in 2 Timothy 3.

The church has become lukewarm. As I visit churches, I

feel like it is a party versus the presence of the Holy Spirit. Sometimes, it feels like the Power of God has left the church. I see men looking around or falling asleep, or I can sense that people are just there, fulfilling their Sunday obligation to check in with the Lord.

Our walk with God is a daily, minute-to-minute, hour-by-hour thing. I have come to a point where I am like Moses in Exodus 33:14-16. *"The Lord replied, "My Presence will go with you, and I will give you rest." Then Moses said to him, "If your Presence does not go with us, do not send us up from here. How will anyone know that you are pleased with me and with your people unless you go with us? What else will distinguish me and your people from all the other people on the face of the earth?"*

I can no longer rely on my own wisdom or strength, nor do I want to do so. I must rely on God's plan and wisdom daily, moment by moment, to carry me through daily life. I am seeking to walk side by side with God daily. I seek obedience in every area of my life and partnering with God while executing my day.

Being obedient to Trinity may mean being called to help others in the Kingdom of God. When we do not act on this, there can be a ripple effect of slowing others down in their walk with God. I want to be clear that we all need to learn skills and become self-sufficient, but as a church, we all need to build one another up, help, and learn the skills necessary to live out our Book of Life purpose to successfully advance Jesus's Kingdom on this earth.

When I tithe or give an offering, I do so very privately. I pray, ask God where that money needs to go, and contact that person privately. I believe very strongly in what Matthew 6:1 teaches, *"Take heed that you do not do your charitable deeds before men, to be seen by them. Otherwise, you have*

no reward from your Father in Heaven. "If I have promised someone something through a directive from God, I will set timelines to accomplish that directive. I gave Matthew 6:1 as an example because we need to take these opportunities to serve our brothers and sisters and unplug ourselves from Satan. Service helps to build faith and trust in other's lives and creates miracles. We sometimes may not understand the roles we are asked to play in any given circumstance, which is why we must carry out the command from the Heavenly Realm when given the order.

I will share one experience, even though I believe it is important to keep these private. One day, I went into a store to find some labels for a few herbal tinctures I had just made. I wanted to get a cheaper price for them. I saw a young man who looked to have a developmental disability possibly. He kept telling the cashier, "I don't have a lot left on my card, and I need to pay with some change. If I don't have enough on my card, I will go out and look for more change in my car." At that moment, I felt the presence of the Lord nudging me to pay for his bill. I was strapped during this paycheck. I waited until the card was declined. At that moment, the cashier rang the young man's card, and she said, "It's declined." I said, "Please put his bill on my card." The boy thanked me and told me he was stressed because he needed everything.

We don't know why God calls us to do those things in those moments. We can either ignore His voice or act on it. I would much rather adhere to His calling and do His will. It's not a matter of doing good work or being rewarded. It's about pleasing Him and being an ambassador for His Kingdom. We lack consistency in this day and age, and if that is a way He can use me daily to be consistent and give, then I am all for that. I have gone without as I have been working through medical issues, and to be able to offer to others in small amounts and believe that I will give in greater amounts down the road is a great feeling. I encourage all of you to work prayerfully with God and do all you can to be obedient to His calling when He asks you to do things for your calling, growing, healing, and giving to others.

CHAPTER 8: Questions for Prayer and Deliverance with the Holy Spirit, Jesus, and the Heavenly Father:

1. What keeps you from consistently following through and completing tasks for others in your life?

2. Are you worried that if you give to others, there will not be enough left over for you or your family?

3. What steps has God asked you to take in your life to heal?

4. What is your life calling that God asks you to complete, but you continue to ignore it? What is one step you can take in each of these areas to walk in alignment with God?

9

―――――

OVERCOMING FEAR

In these last days, I want to encourage you to be at peace and give your burdens and concerns to Jesus. Matthew 5:13-16 states, *"You are the salt of the earth; but if the salt loses its flavor, how shall it be seasoned? It is then good for nothing but to be thrown out and trampled underfoot by men. You are the light of the world. A city that is set on a hill cannot be hidden."* The mission you are asked to carry out for the Lord is to submit and to be consistent in accomplishing the deeds He is asking you to accomplish for your life and others.

We cannot control what others do not follow through on. Ultimately, they will be held accountable if they do not play their part. However, our jobs are to quiet ourselves to get our orders so "we can be the salt of the earth" and to be the light of Jesus for others while walking the earth.

I can think of two situations I went through while writing this book where I needed several people to follow through to help me. They did not follow through. Did it hurt? Yes. However, I had to turn that over to Jesus, and I had to lean further into Him and trust Him for my provision in a time of great distress. I was also led to help others with their life purpose.

I was in tremendous fear at the time. I felt defeated. However, this experience gave me time to slow down, re-evaluate, and trust God. It gave me further validation that committing myself to this path was correct. Living a life for Christ will not always be easy. When walking this path, pride must be put out of the way. Prayer and being in the Word must be our weapons of warfare to combat the enemy, especially when we want to delay orders from the Heavenly Realm. I cannot stress it enough. We will have to be battle-ready and going through these experiences at times will make us warriors for God's Kingdom.

A passage in 2 Timothy 1:7 tells us, ***"For God has not given us a spirit of fear but of power and of love and of a sound mind."*** I have learned that when we battle the Spirit of fear, we have the power and authority in Jesus' name to command that Spirit of fear to leave. I know that when I get into stress or fear, I forget that I have the mind of Christ. Jesus is there to walk side by side with me and provide a solution to any problem. I need to enter into quiet and prayer. 1 Corinthians 2:14-16 states, ***"The natural man does not receive the things of the Spirit of God, for they are foolishness to him; nor can he know them, because they are spiritually discerned. But he who is spiritual judges all things, yet he himself is rightly judged by no one. For "who has known the mind of the LORD that he may instruct Him?" But we have the mind of Christ."***

In closing, do the best you can daily. We are one with Christ and our Heavenly Father. All we have to do is quiet ourselves and wait patiently for His answers.

. . .

CHAPTER 9: Questions for Prayer and Deliverance with the Holy Spirt, Jesus, and the Heavenly Father:

1. What are the main things in your life that you need to repent from doing that could be keeping you from living your life purpose?

2. What are the top three fears that hold you back from working on yourself daily and being obedient to what God calls you to do for yourself, those you love, and others?

3. Meditate on James 2:14, which states, **"What does it profit, my brethren, if someone says he has faith but does not have works? Can faith save him? If a brother or sister is naked and destitute of daily food, and one of you says to them, 'Depart in peace, be warmed and filled, but you do not give them the things which are needed for the body, what does it profit?' Thus, also faith by itself, if it does not have works, is dead."** Ask yourself the following question with the Holy Spirit:

a. Where can you be asked to give in small amounts? It can be of your time, money, talents, or helping someone step to the next level to help them serve the Kingdom of God more effectively.

b. What steps can you immediately take and not be in fear?

OBEDIENCE SCRIPTURES:

Meditate and pray with Trinity to help you become free. Become more obedient in your walk with the Lord daily to walk in your Book of Life Purpose for the Kingdom of God. Sit quietly and enjoy your time with God, Jesus, and the Holy Spirit. May these hand-picked scriptures assist you in deliverance and walking in the Spirit, in Jesus' name.

- **Proverbs 9:10** – *"The fear of the Lord is the beginning of wisdom, and the knowledge of the Holy One is understanding."*
- **2 Samuel 22:2** – *He said, "The Lord is my rock and my fortress and my deliverer."*
- **2 Timothy 3:16** – *"All Scripture is breathed by God and profitable for teaching, by reproof, for correction, and for training in righteousness."*
- **Exodus 14:5-6** – *"Now therefore, if you will indeed obey My voice and keep My covenant, then you shall be a special treasure to Me above all people; for all the earth is Mine. And you shall be to Me a kingdom of*

priests and a holy nation. These are the words which you shall speak to the children of Israel."

- **Matthew 7:21** – *"Not everyone who says to Me, 'Lord, Lord,' shall enter the kingdom of Heaven, but he who does the will of My Father in Heaven."*

- **Luke 11:28** – *"But He said, "More than that, blessed are those who hear the word of God and keep it!"*

- **John 14:21** – "He who has My commandments and keeps them, it is he who loves Me. And he who loves Me will be loved by My Father, and I will love him and manifest Myself to him."

- **Acts 5:29** – "But Peter and the other apostles answered and said: 'We ought to obey God rather than men.'"

- **James 1-22:24** – "But be doers of the word, and not hearers only, deceiving yourselves. For if anyone is a hearer of the word and not a doer, he is like a man observing his natural face in a mirror; for he observes himself, goes away, and immediately forgets what kind of man he was."

- **1 John 2:3-6** – *"Now by this we know that we know Him, if we keep His commandments. He who says, 'I know Him,' and does not keep His commandments, is a liar, and the truth is not in him. But whoever keeps His word, truly the love of God is perfected in him. By this we know that we are in Him. He who says he abides in Him ought himself also to walk just as He walked."*

- **Deuteronomy 5:33** – *"You shall walk in all the ways which the LORD your God has commanded you, that you may live and that it may be well with you, and that you may prolong your days in the land which you shall possess."*

- **1 Corinthians 15:58** – *"Therefore, my beloved brethren, be ye stedfast, unmoveable, always abounding in the work of the Lord, forasmuch as ye know that your labour is not in vain in the Lord."*
- **John 15:16** – *"You did not choose Me, but I chose you and appointed you that you should go and bear fruit, and that your fruit should remain, that whatever you ask the Father in My name He may give you."*
- **Romans 12:2** – *"And do not be conformed to this world, but be transformed by the renewing of your mind, that you may prove what is that good and acceptable and perfect will of God."*
- **1 Kings 2:3** – *"And keep the charge of the Lord your God: to walk in His ways, to keep His statutes, His commandments, His judgments, and His testimonies, as it is written in the Law of Moses, that you may prosper in all that you do and wherever you turn."*
- **Psalms 128:1** – *"Blessed is every one who fears the Lord, who walks in His ways."*
- **Romans 8:14** – *"For as many as are led by the Spirit of God, these are sons of God."*
- **1 John 2:17** – *"And the world is passing away, and the lust of it; but he who does the will of God abides forever."*
- **John 15:5-8** – *"I am the vine, you are the branches. He who abides in Me, and I in him, bears much fruit; for without Me you can do nothing. If anyone does not abide in Me, he is cast out as a branch and is withered; and they gather them and throw them into the fire, and they are burned. If you abide in Me, and My words abide in you, you will ask what you desire, and it shall be done for you. By this My Father is*

glorified, that you bear much fruit; so you will be My disciples."

- **Luke 10:27** – *So he answered and said, "You shall love the Lord your God with all your heart, with all your soul, with all your strength, and with all your mind,' and 'your neighbor as yourself."*

ABOUT THE AUTHOR

ABOUT THE AUTHOR

Jeffrey Tierney is an ex-new ager, now a Christian, with a background in social services and transpersonal/parapsychology. He is the author of *Get Your Act Together: A 30-Day Account- ability Journal and The Love Well Letters.*

Theme of Work:

Jeffrey's 20 plus years of experience in social work and his history in the darkness of the new age/occult enables him to discuss the importance of accountability in today's world. Accountability brings us closer to Christ and one another. By holding ourselves accountable, love, connection, and intimacy are increased with those we love.

Personal Life:

Jeffrey lives and works in Omaha, Nebraska, where he enjoys reading Scripture, praying, using nutrition and supplements, exercising, helping others, making positive, witty t-shirts, watching Husker Football, and growing closer to Christ — plus general tomfoolery.

You can visit Jeff's website at jeffreytierney.org

"Don't wait until you are near death to prioritize love and accountability." Jeffrey T. Tierney